A Special Gift For:

_____

From:

_____

This book is dedicated to the silent voice within each of us that prompts us to do what is right.

Finders Keepers?

A True Story

Robert Arnett

Robert Arnett
Illustrated by Smita Turakhia

Smita Turakhia

INDIA UNVEILED
Children's Series

Vol. I

Atman Press

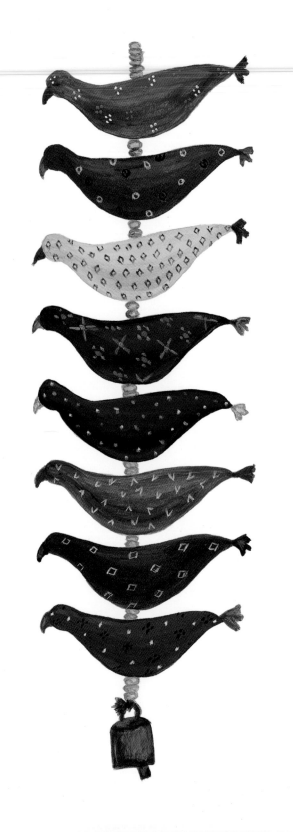

Text ©2003
Robert Arnett

Illustrations ©2003
Smita Turakhia

Published by Atman Press
PMB 345
2525 Auburn Avenue
Columbus, Georgia 31906-1376
(800) 563-4198
www.atmanpress.com

Editors
Smita Turakhia
Doug Glener

Maps: Scott McIntyre

Printed and bound in South Korea.
First Edition - 2003

ISBN: 0-9652900-2-6
Library of Congress Control Number: 2003103991

Publisher's Cataloging-in-Publication Data
Arnett, Robert, 1942 -

Finders Keepers?
by Robert Arnett
Illustrated by Smita Turakhia

32 p. 27.94 cm.
Includes glossary, index and
pronunciation guide

Summary: Emphasizes important
universal values for children.

1. India — Social life and customs
2. India — Religion and culture
3. India — Description and travel
4. India — Art

J 915.4

Contents

A Warm Welcome

In India, a *toran** is hung over a doorway to welcome God and guests. *Torans* made of fresh flowers and leaves can be seen all across the country.

In the state of Rajasthan* in northwest India where the story took place, *torans* are made of fabric and then decorated with brightly colored embroidery, appliqués, and mirrors. The cloth pennants that hang down from *torans* represent leaves from sacred trees.

This *toran* welcomes you to *Finders Keepers?* As you step through its portal, may you be blessed to always seek truth.

The Bus Ride

It is hard to look out a window and see the sights of India when every time your bus goes over a bump, you bounce so high off your seat you almost hit your head on the roof! But there I was, bouncing along on my way to Mt. Abu,* a small town on a mountain in the state of Rajasthan.

RAJASTHAN

Jaisalmer

Jaipur

Pushkar

Ajmer

Ranakpur

Mt. Abu

Some adventurous men and boys who could not get seats inside the bus rode on top with the luggage. Though I would have enjoyed the cool breeze and a panoramic view from the top, I preferred to stay where I was!

INDIA

9

The bus was packed with people and their belongings. Most of the women were dressed in brightly colored *saris.** Many of the men were wearing traditional clothes and had colorful turbans on their heads. They had full mustaches that curled at each end. The rainbow colors of their clothing gave the inside of the bus a festive look.

Though most passengers were strangers to each other, we quickly became like a big family traveling together. Some people shared food, and others passed young children and babies around, perhaps to give the mothers a rest.
The children were happy and contented to be
entertained by total strangers — even
by me!

I knew I was far from my home in the
United States when I watched a man
take off his turban. To my surprise,
I saw that on top of his head was his
lunch. It was several flat pieces of
bread called *chapatis** and a few
carrots. I had never seen anyone
use a turban and his head as
a lunchbox!

11

We stopped for lunch at a roadside rest stop. As I got off the bus, I saw several people pointing up at a tree. I was amazed to see large bats hanging upside down from the tree limbs, roosting during the day. The harmless fruit bats, called flying foxes, looked like special effects from a vampire movie.

At a nearby food stall, a man was boiling milk mixed with sugar in a large cauldron over an open fire. I bought a glass of hot milk that he topped with some cream skimmed from the surface of the steaming liquid. To cool it for me, a boy skillfully poured it from one glass to another. The delicious drink tasted like a milkshake. The savory snacks that were piled high looked appealing and I bought some to munch on for the rest of the trip.

I Meet a Monk

Our rickety old bus chugged up the rugged mountain and finally we arrived at Mt. Abu. I was staying in a Hindu* monastery that is called an *ashram.**

An old monk greeted me at the door. He was a tall man with a long, gray beard and gray hair. He wore a wool sweater, a cotton wrap-around skirt called a *lungi,** and a pair of sandals. I wondered how he stayed warm on such a cold winter's day. What attracted me most was the friendly sparkle in his eyes.

After dinner, we sat around a small fire. The monk told me that he had spent many years as a hermit living in a forest and praying to God. "The Lord is my provider. I don't need to own anything to be happy," he said to me.

As I lay in bed before I fell asleep, I thought about something else the monk had said: "All men are my brothers and every woman is my mother."

How beautiful to look upon EVERY and being as dear to you as

ONE you meet as part of your family a brother, a sister, or a parent.

Tour of Mt. Abu

The next morning, I took a bus tour to visit some of the temples in Mt. Abu.

On the way, I saw some nuns and monks of the Jain* religion walking down the road. In one hand, they were carrying their food containers in a white cotton cloth.

With their other hand, they were sweeping the ground ahead of them so that they would not hurt any insects, or even seeds, by accidentally stepping on them.

Their mouths were covered with a small cloth to avoid swallowing even the tiniest insects floating in the air. Because Jains believe that everything has a soul, they respect and protect all forms of life.

The highlight of my bus tour was seeing the famous Jain Dilwara* Temples that are said to have the finest marble carvings in the world. The delicate designs on the inside of the huge marble domes made the ceiling look like it was covered with snowflakes.

We also went to a Hindu temple that had a statue of Shiva.* Shiva is a part of the Hindu Trinity* and represents God's activity within the created universe. To Hindus, he also represents God's power that takes all things back to their origin when their stay in the world is completed.

Though Hinduism* believes in only one God, it gives names and forms to God's many aspects to help us better understand His mysterious power and intelligence. Thinking about what the statue of Shiva symbolizes, I realized that Hinduism, like Christianity, believes in a Trinity.

Finders Keepers?

The last stop on the tour was at a Hindu temple built on the highest peak in Rajasthan. While going up the path that led to the temple, I stopped to buy some postcards. As I walked away, I felt someone tapping my elbow.

A small, dark-haired boy was standing behind me. To my surprise, in his outstretched hand was my wallet. I must have dropped it when I bought the postcards.

I offered the boy a reward for returning my wallet, but he would not accept it. I even tried to put some money into his hands, but he put them behind his back. Again, I made an attempt to reward him for his honesty, but he refused. I could not understand why the boy would not take the money.

I went up to a man who could speak English to see if he could help me. "This boy found my wallet and returned it to me. Please explain to him that I want to reward him for his honesty."

The man began talking to the boy in their language. After a few minutes, the boy did most of the talking. I was beginning to wonder if either of them understood me.

Then the man turned to me and said, "This boy does not understand why you should give him any money for returning to you what is yours. The idea of accepting a reward for doing a good deed makes no sense to him."

Finders keepers? No way!

Which Way?

That night in the *ashram,* I thought of the little boy's honesty again. It would have taken him many years to earn the amount of money in the wallet, yet he was not tempted to keep it. He listened to his conscience.*

The dictionary defines conscience as the recognition within us of right and wrong regarding what we do and why we do it. It urges us towards right action. Some people believe that our conscience, or inner voice, is the silent voice of God trying to guide us and that if we listen to it, we will always do what is right.

To do what is right in any situation is one of the most important principles of Indian culture, and is one way to explain their concept of *dharma.** It means to "Do what you ought to do, not what you want to do."

Think of the little boy who found my wallet. He never considered keeping the wallet for himself when he knew that it belonged to someone else. He returned it because it was the right thing to do and not because he hoped to get a reward. To him, his reward was in knowing that he had done what was right. And that's the best reward of all!

Your Journey Begins

I hope you enjoyed traveling with me to India. I enjoyed traveling with you. Now it is time for me to say *namaste.** Namaste* is how many Indians greet each other instead of saying "hello" and "goodbye."

While uttering "*namaste,*" they place the fingers and palms of both hands together in front of the chest and slightly bow the head. It is also called a *pranam** and is a gesture of humility and respect.

The respect that people show to each other when they *pranam* is one of the things I love most about India. In the Sanskrit* language, to *pranam* or to say *namaste* means "the God in me bows to the God in you" or "my soul bows to your soul."

It expresses the belief that God is present deep within each of us — that the skin color, the race, or the religion does not alter the divine soul-image of God within each person.

Once we believe and understand this, we will never do anything to anyone that we would not do to God. So dear ones, let your journey begin.

Life is a journey.

Let your inner voice be your guide.

Treat all who cross your path with love and kindness.

Gallantly, reach for the stars.

Jog Your Memory

ashram. A Hindu monastery; a residence of a spiritual teacher and his students.

Christianity. The religion based on the teachings of Jesus Christ. Their scripture is the Bible.

conscience. The recognition within us of what is right and wrong moral behavior.

dharma. Righteous action (Hinduism). To do what is right, regardless of the circumstances.

hermit. A person who lives away from other people to seek God.

Hindu. A follower of Hinduism. Hindus believe in only one God, which can express Itself in many forms.

Hinduism. The largest religion of India. Their religion has many scriptures, of which the Vedas are the most ancient.

Jains. Followers of Jainism. Mahavir is the founder. Their religion began in India. Their scriptures are the Agam Sutras.

lungi. A cloth wrapped around the waist like a sarong, worn by Indian men.

monastery. A house or place where monks and nuns live.

namaste. Hindu greeting for "hello" and "goodbye." It means "my soul bows to your soul."

pranam. A custom of placing both hands together and bowing one's head when greeting someone with *namaste*.

Sanskrit. The religious and literary language of ancient India. Sanskrit is the oldest surviving language in the world and influenced many languages of modern Europe.

sari. An 18 foot long cloth worn by women that wraps around the waist to form a skirt and then drapes over the shoulder or head like a shawl. It is worn with a tight fitting blouse.

Shiva. Hindu diety who represents God's activity within creation to include dissolving everything back into its origin when its stay in creation is completed. See Trinity.

toran. A hanging used over a doorway in India as a sign of welcome, believed to bring good luck.

Trinity.
Christianity: The threefold personality of God — the Father, the Son, and the Holy Ghost.
Hinduism: God's three roles in creation become the Trinity — Brahma, The Creator; Vishnu, The Preserver; and Shiva, The Dissolver. Brahma represents God's power as Creator of the universe; Vishnu represents God's intelligence in creation that holds the universe in balance; and Shiva represents God's activity within the created universe. Shiva dissolves everything in the universe back into its origin when its stay in creation is completed.

Oh, See Can You Say

ashram: ASH-rum
chapatis: chuh-PAH-tees
dharma: DHUR-muh
Dilwara: deel-WAH-rah
Hindu: HIN-doo
Jain: Jane
lungi: LOONG-gee
Mt. Abu: Mount AH-boo

namaste: NUM-ah-stay
pranam: pruh-NAHM
Rajasthan: RAH-juh-stahn
Sanskrit: SAN-skrit
saris: SAH-rees
Shiva: SHEE-vah
toran: TOH-run

Food For Thought

1. Would you do something just to please someone else when your inner voice says it is wrong?

   When we do the right thing, we feel so good about ourselves that we do not need to seek the approval of our friends.

2. Do you think you should be paid to help around the house for doing things like keeping your room clean or washing the dishes? Is it not your responsibility as a part of the family to help with the chores?

People, Places, and Things

appliqués, decorations where one material is sewed or applied to another, 7

ashram, Hinduism, monastery I visited in Mt. Abu, 14, 28, 30

bats, "flying foxes," 12

chapatis, thin, flat pieces of bread, 11, 30

Christianity, the religion based on the teachings of Jesus Christ, 19, 28

conscience, inner voice of truth within each of us, 24, 28

dharma, Hinduism, righteous action, 24, 28, 30

Dilwara Temples, Jain temples I visited in Rajasthan, 18, 30

divine, having the qualities of God, 26

hermit, a person who lives away from others to seek God, 15, 28

Hindu, a follower of Hinduism, the largest religion of India, 14, 19, 28, 30

humility, not seeing oneself as being more important than others, 26

Jains, followers of Jainism, 18, 28, 30

lungi, Indian skirt worn by men, 14, 28, 30

monastery, a house or place where monks and nuns live, 14, 28

monk, a man who lives in a monastery to seek God, 14, 15, 18

Mt. Abu, town I visited in Rajasthan, 9, 14, 18, 30

namaste, Indian greeting, 26, 28, 30

nun, a woman who lives in a monastery to seek God, 18

pranam, gesture of respect, 26, 29, 30

Rajasthan, state in northwest India, 7, 9, 30

Sanskrit, ancient religious and literary language of India, 26, 30

saris, women's clothing, India, 11, 29, 30

Shiva, Hindu deity, 19, 29, 30

soul, the higher essence of humankind, as distinct from the body, 26

temples, Hindu and Jain places of worship I visited in Mt. Abu, 18, 19, 20

toran, a hanging over a doorway in India, 6, 7, 29, 30

Trinity, threefold personality of God, 19, 29

turban, cloth wrapped around head to form headdress, 11

wallet, I lost and was returned to me, 20, 22, 24

The Author

Robert Arnett, a native of Columbus, Georgia, has a Master's Degree in History from Indiana University. He has had an avid interest in India for over 30 years. From 1988 to the present, he has made five trips to India and spent over 19 months there studying art, culture, and religion while living with Indian families.

He is the author of the highly acclaimed book *India Unveiled*, a travelogue illustrated with award-winning photography, which has won the Small Press Book Award for Best Travel Book of the Year and the Benjamin Franklin Award for the Best Travel Essay of the Year. It is probably the only book ever published in the Western world to have been officially recognized by a Prime Minister of India.

Mr. Arnett has lectured widely throughout North America, including the Smithsonian Institute, Harvard and Yale Universities, and The Explorers Club. He was a speaker at the Parliament of the World's Religions held in Cape Town, South Africa. He has been interviewed on National Public Radio, Voice of America, South African Broadcasting Corporation, and various television programs. He has also given numerous presentations at schools, libraries, community organizations, temples, and churches.

To arrange a presentation in your city, please contact Mr. Arnett directly at 800-563-4198, or email him at robertarnett@mindspring.com. For more information about *India Unveiled*, please visit www.india-unveiled.com.

The Illustrator

The paintings in *Finders Keepers?* come from the hand of Smita Turakhia, a children's illustrator who has devoted herself to bringing India's cultural heritage to life through art.

Mrs. Turakhia's portfolio includes illustrations for *The Journey to the Truth*, an award-winning CD-ROM that depicted for the first time the messages and metaphors of the Bhagavad Gita in the Warli folk art style of India.

A graduate of Nirmala Niketan, Mumbai, India, Mrs. Turakhia also studied fine arts for two years at the University of New Mexico, Albuquerque, and studied under one of India's Gold Medal artists. She currently resides in Lake Jackson, Texas with her husband and two daughters. You may contact Mrs. Turakhia at turakhiasmita@yahoo.com.